Best wishes at
Christmas
Dave & Nina
1983

TAKE MY JOKES, PLEASE

By
Henny Youngman

RICHARDSON & SNYDER
1983

ISBN: 0-943940-05-2
Library of Congress in Publication Data:

1. Title: TAKE MY JOKES, PLEASE
2. Author: Henny Henny Youngman
3. Humor, contemporary American
4. Psychology of American behavior patterns

TAKE MY JOKES, PLEASE

A Christian visiting the Holy Land
struck up a conversation with a Israeli.
"I'm really surprised that you and the Arabs
can't get along together peacefully."
"My dear man," said the Israeli,
"the Jews are a very argumentative people.
The only thing you can get two Jews
to agree upon is
what a third Jew should give to charity."

◆◆◆

The voice of the stewardess
on the Israeli charter airliner
came over the loudspeaker:
"Welcome aboard. Your hostesses are
Mrs. Dora Fein and Mrs. Fay Hershberg
and, of course, my son, the pilot."

◢ ◥

A fellow was taken to a nudist colony
for the first time.
Finally one blond beauty struck his eye,
and his host said to him,
"How does she impress you?"
"Gee!
How I'd like to see her with a sweater on."

Mrs. Moskowitz loved chicken soup.
One evening she was spooning it up
when three of her husband's friends came in.
"Mrs. Moskowitz," the spokesman said,
"we are here to tell you that your husband
Izzy has been killed in an automobile accident."
Mrs. Moskowitz continued eating her soup.
Again they told her.
Still no reaction.
"Look," said the puzzled speaker,
"We are telling you that your husband is dead."
She went right on with the soup.
"Gentlemen," she said between mouthfuls,
"soon as I'm finished with this chicken soup,
you gonna hear some scream!"

‡‡‡

Old man Krastenfeld lay on his deathbed
for months and finally passed away.
Two weeks later,
the relatives gathered like vultures
to hear the reading of the will.
The lawyer tore open an envelope,
drew out a piece of paper and read:
"Being of sound mind,
I spent every dime before I died."

A guy gets a new pet,
a little pussy cat,
and he falls in love with it.
The pussy cat follows him everywhere,
and he is just crazy about his little pet.
The man wins a free trip to Paris,
and he leaves the pussy cat with his brother.
Two weeks later he calls his brother from Paris.
"How is my little pussy cat?"
The brother says, "Your cat died."
The guy is stunned and says,
"Why did you have to tell me like that?
You could have told me
the pussy was on the roof
and broke its leg.
Then I could have gotten used to the idea
gradually."
The brother says,
"Forgive me, I'm sorry."
"Okay, I forgive you. By the way, how is Mom?"
The brother says,
"She's on the roof."

Mrs. Ponce de Leon says to her husband,
"Ponce, you're going to Miami without me?"

TAKE MY JOKES, *PLEASE*

We're sure living in a fast world.
Take the doctor who told his patient
on Monday,
"Stop eating red meat!
In your condition it's not good for you."
On Tuesday the doctor told him
to resume eating red meat,
that it *was* good for him.
The patient looks confused and asks,
"But, Doc, what goes?
Yesterday you said
that red meat was bad for me,
and today you say
that red meat is good for me."
The doctor said, "Listen,
you'd be surprised how medicine
has progressed in the last 24 hours!"

Guy: "I want you to be
the mother of my children...."
Gal: "How many you got?"

I went to a celebrity charity ball....
I was the only one I never heard of.

◊ ◇ ◊

A fellow with a swollen wrist
was advised by his doctor
to go home and keep the wrist
in a pail of extremely hot water
for twelve hours.
He obeyed the advice,
but instead of his wrist getting better,
his whole body began to swell.
His maid spoke up and said,
"Cold water is better than hot."
He put his wrist in cold water
and all his swelling,
including the wrist, stopped.
Now he was angry,
so he called up his doctor and shouted,
"What kind of a doctor are you?
You told me to put my wrist in hot water,
and my whole body swelled.
My maid told me to put it in cold water,
and I got better immediately."
The doctor replied,
"I can't understand it;
my maid said hot water."

"How is your wife?"
"Compared to who?"

♦◆♦

Jewish man talking to his friend,
"If I live I'll see you Tuesday.
If I don't I'll see you Wednesday."

Edwin Lehman,
Ship 'n Shore's dashing West Coast Manager,
delivers this delightful dash of drollery:
A sign in a Brooklyn candy store read:
CIGARETTES 60 CENTS A PACKAGE.
By 8:00 in the morning
a line had already formed all around the block.
Markowitz pushed his way to the front
of the line.
Polowski, a big burly steel worker
grabbed him and shouted,
"Get to the rear of the line."
A few minutes later,
Markowitz pushed his way through the crowd,
got to the door,
and the big Polack shoved him away.
Markowitz tried again
and again Polowski shoved him back.
Finally Markowitz said,
"Look, if you push me, once more —
I ain't gonna open the store!"

Berkowitz, a salesman,
while driving through the Negev desert,
saw an Arab lying on the sand.
Berkowitz rushed to the man's side
and lifted him up.
The Arab whispered,
"Water, Effendi, Water."
"This is Kismet," exclaimed Berkowitz.
"Are you in luck.
I happen to have in my suitcase
the finest selection of ties you ever saw."
"No," wailed the Arab,
"Water! Water!"
"These ties you could see right now
in the King David Hotel –
$15 apiece, for you only $10!"
"Please, Effendi, I need water!"
"Look, you seem like a nice person.
I'm known all over the Negev as 'Honest Abe'."
Whatever kind of ties you like –
silk, wool, crepe –
you can have what you want ...
$8 each!"
"I need w-w-water!"
"All right, you drive a hard bargain.
Tell you what – take your pick.
Two for $10."
"Pul-ese, give me water!"

"Oh, you want water? said Berkowitz,
"why didn't you say so?
All you gotta do is crawl 500 feet
to that sand dune,
hang a right for a quarter of a mile,
you'll come to Poopy's Pyramid Club.
He'll give you all the water you want!"
The Arab slowly crawled to the sand dune,
turned right
and with his last remaining strength
came to the door of the club.
Poopy, the owner, was standing out front.
"Water, Water!"
begged the Arab.
"You want water.
You came to the right place!
I got well water,
seltzer water,
whatever water you want,
I got on the inside.
The only thing is –
you can't go in without a tie."

◆◆◆

There's nothing wrong with our foreign policy
that faith, hope and clarity couldn't cure!

A doctor was awakened by a call
from a patient he had never heard of.
It was a brutal, blizzardy night out,
and the medico didn't want to go on the call,
but his wife said to him,
"Why, darling,
remember the oath of Hippocrates.
You must go to the sick and wounded."
So the doctor got up from his warm bed
and went through the snow and ice;
his car broke down;
he walked through the blizzard
the remaining few miles
and came to the home of the patient.
He examined him and said to his patient,
"Have your immediate family,
relatives and friends come here at once."
The doctor got home at 6 a.m.
His wife tried to console him.
"Darling," she said,
"That's why you were ordained
to help the sick and wounded.
How did you find the patient?"
"I told him to have his immediate family,
relatives and friends come to him at once."
"Is he that bad?" cried the wife.
"No, in fact,
there is nothing the matter with him.

But I am not going to be the only sucker
out on a night like this."

Nathan and Ira had been partners for years,
and now Ira lay dying.
Nathan stood at his hospital bedside.
"I have a confession to make" said Ira,
"I robbed our firm of $100,000.
I sold the secret formula to our competitors.
I took the letter from your desk
that your wife needed to get her divorce.
And Nathan, I...."
"It's all right," said his partner.
"It was me that poisoned you!"

A wife rushed into the police station
with this complaint:
"My husband beats me up every day.
I am such a nervous wreck
that I've lost thirty-five pounds."
The police captain said,
"Do you want him arrested?"
"No, not yet.
I want to lose fifty pounds more first."

Two young men and one very old man
were discussing in what manner
they would like to die.
One man said,
"I'd like to be shot up in the latest missile,
and though it would kill me,
I would feel that I went higher in space
than any other man.
That is the way I would like to die."
The second man said,
"I'd like to go down to the depths of the sea
in the heaviest submarine
and look through the portholes
at the denizens of the deep.
And when I had my fill,
I would let the submarine be my tomb."
They turned to the old man and said,
"How would you like to die?"
"I'd like to be shot by a jealous husband."

‡‡‡

A woman wrapped in saran wrap
to take weight off.
Her husband comes home,
sees her and says,
"Left-overs again!"

★ ★ ★

A wife told her husband
that the doctor said she was not too well
and needed the ocean breezes.
So he fanned her with a herring.

■ ■ ■

A tourist saw a loafer leaning against a post
and said to him,
"Why don't you get a job,
save your money,
then invest your money?
Then when you become rich
you won't have to work any more."
"Why should I go to all that trouble?
I'm not working now."

†††

I would have had a wonderful time
in Las Vegas
if it wasn't for the temperature.
The sun was too hot,
and the dice were too cold.

◊ ◇ ◊

Am I forgetful?...
Last night I forgot the Alamo!

☎

Rutkin and Sakolsky were walking home
from a lodge meeting.
"So what is your son doing for a living?"
asked Rutkin.
"He got some crazy idea in college.
He studied to be a psychiatrist."
"How is he doing?"
"Not bad!"
"Why not?" answered Sakolsky.
"I understand these fellers pick up plenty
of change that falls behind the couch!"

▷∘◁

I have another brother-in-law
who is an idiot.
During the black-out in New York
he was stuck on an escalator for four hours.
When I asked him why he didn't walk down
he said,
"I was on my way up."

□ □ □

Americans are getting stronger.
Twenty years ago it took two people
to carry ten dollars worth of groceries.
Today a five-year-old can do it.

▷∘◁

Psychiatrist –
A Jewish doctor
who can't stand the sight of blood.

‡‡‡

How times have changed.
Remember 30 years ago,
when a juvenile delinquent was a kid
with an overdue library book?

■ ■ ■

Seymour Grand,
New Jersey's grandiloquent sandwich gourmet,
provides customers with this gift of humor:
Sokolow, aged 75, rushed into a doctor's office.
"You gotta give me a shot,
so I should be young again," he pleaded.
"I got a date with a young chicken tonight!"
"Just a minute," said the physician,
"You're 75 years old.
There's nothing I can do for you!"
"But doctor," exclaimed the old man,
"my friend, Rosen, is 85,
and he says he has sex three times a week."
"All right," advised the doctor,
"So *you say* it too!"

□ □ □

Two friends went to a summer resort together.
A few months later one asked the other.
"Do you remember that widow we met?
Did you make love to her,
pose as me,
use my name,
and even give her my address?"
"Yes, Bill, I made violent love to her,
and as a gag I posed as you
and gave her your name and address.
I didn't think you would mind."
"Mind? A lawyer called on me today."
"A lawyer called on you today?"
"Yes. She died
and left me two hundred thousand dollars."

My wife has already informed me
she doesn't want me to be President.
Says she couldn't stand having all the neighbors
know exactly what I make.

Henny Youngman says to the manager
when entering a restaurant,
"Give me a table near a waiter, please."

A couple is driving to Miami Beach
in a brand new car.
As they're driving,
he puts his hand on her knee.
She says,
"We're married now,
you can go a little farther."
So he went to Ft. Lauderdale.

Two Jewish ladies were in a building.
One says to the other,
"Do you see what's going on
in the Middle East, Iran and Afghanistan?"
"I don't see anything.
I live in the back of the building."

☆ ☆ ☆

We went for a ride,
and my wife went through a red light.
I said,
"Didn't you see that red light?"
She said,
"So what?
You see one red light,
you've seen them all!"

A citizen's viewpoint:
"I vote only for a man who runs for re-election.
When a man runs for re-election,
it means he is honest;
it means he has not been able to put his hand
in the till the first time."

A fellow, to stay in business,
always insisted on having his checks
dated ahead,
so they let him do it.
But even with that advantage,
he died,
and his tombstone reads:
"Here lies the body of Morris Blivitz –
died April 15,
as of May 1."

There is a town in the Middle West
that has had the same population,
to a person,
for the last fifty years,
because every time a child is born
somebody has to leave town.

This is an era of compromise.
At a party one evening
one of the guests said to a girl,
"Will you come up to my studio tonight?"
Indignantly she replied,
"How dare you?
You don't even know my name.
However, since you seem so anxious,
I'll give you a sporting chance."
She clenched her fist and said,
"If you tell me what I have in my hand,
I'll go to your studio with you tonight.
Now, what have I got in my hand?"
He replied, "An elephant."
"That's close enough," came her reply.

Here it is election time,
and once again isn't it amazing
how many wide open spaces there are –
entirely surrounded by teeth.

ISRAELI NAVY SLOGAN
DON'T GIVE UP THE SHIP –
SELL IT!

†††

19

We asked a zoologist how porcupines have sex.
"Carefully,
very carefully!"

Janovitz was living it up
at a Ft. Lauderdale senior citizens dance,
and he lost his wallet containing $600.
"Excuse me," he announced,
standing on a chair,
"but I lost my wallet with $600 in it.
To the man that finds it I will give $50."
A voice from the rear shouted,
"I'll give $75."

★ ★ ★

It looks like he took
an Evelyn Woods speed eating course.

†††

My father was never home;
he was always drinking booze.
He saw a sign saying,
"Drink Canada Dry!"
So he went up there.

I was in the supermarket the other day.
I thought I was in church.
Women were walking up the aisles saying,
"Oh, My God!"

Did you hear about the expectant father
who wanted to name the baby Oscar
because it was his best performance
of the year?

The lawyer stood before the family
of the recently deceased Hershel Ostrow
and read aloud his will.
"To my dear wife,
I leave my house, fifty acres of land
and one million dollars.
To my son, Rubie,
I leave my two cars and $200,000.00.
To my daughter, Sarah,
I leave my yacht and $200,000.00.
And to my brother-in-law,
who always insisted that health
is better than wealth,
I leave my sun lamp."

☆ ☆ ☆

I bet 9 out of 10 I.R.S. auditors
come from broken homes.

‡‡‡

A Lufthansa jet goes down
and lands in the ocean ten miles from Germany.
The captain announces over the microphone,
"Ladies and gentlemen,
all those who can swim
use the emergency exit
and start swimming –
you are only ten miles from shore.
All those who can't swim…
thank you for flying Lufthansa!"

†††

A little Jewish man died in a town.
He must have been a horrible man
because no one wanted to say a good word
at his funeral,
not even a local rabbi,
so they asked a rabbi in the next town.
He said, "I didn't like him either,
but I'll say a few words."
He gets up at the funeral and says,
"His brother was worse."

Did you here the one about the ministers
who formed a bowling team?
Called themselves the Holy Rollers?

He asked the doctor to perform a vasectomy,
but the doctor said,
"Let sleeping dogs lie."

■ ■ ■

It's one of those highly ethical colleges
that doesn't believe in buying
its football players.
All it gives them is room, board
and $200 a week toward their textbooks.

◇ ◇ ◇

I watched a new car roll off the assembly line.
It's amazing.
They start out with little pieces
that roll down the assembly line,
and thousands of men and a million dollars
worth of machinery put everything together.
Finally, a shiny new car emerges.
Then a woman buys it,
and turns it into little pieces again.

A guy has been in the army for four years.
He's going through his old belongings,
and he finds a ticket for a pair of shoes
that he had left at the shoemaker
before he went to war.
Figuring he'd take a chance,
he goes down to the shoemaker and says,
"I put my shoes in to be fixed four years ago
before I went into the army.
Do you still have them?
The shoemaker takes the ticket
and goes into the back room.
He comes out and says,
"They'll be ready Tuesday."

□ □ □

A couple is visiting Las Vegas.
The wife gambles all night long,
playing every game in the casino.
At dawn the husband says, "Let's go to bed."
She says, "No, I don't like the odds!"

† † †

We got a new garbage disposal –
my brother-in-law.
He'll eat anything.

Things could be much worse. . . .
I could be one of my creditors.

††††

Have you seen *Mommie Dearest*? . . .
My wife was technical advisor.

Mother says to her son,
"Come on and get out of bed."
Her son says,
"I don't want to go to work –
the people around me don't like me."
The mother says,
"Get up, Ronald,
you have to get to work –
you're the President of the United States!"

■ ■ ■

Took a physical for some life insurance. . . .
All they would give me was fire and theft.

If you're not on pills or booze,
people think you're overconfident.

◊ ◇ ◊

This Irish guy dropped dead.
Who should tell the wife – and how?
A guy volunteered.
He knocked at the door
– a lady came out –
and he said,
"Is this the widow Ryan?"
"I'm not the widow Ryan."
"Wait until you see
what they're dragging in the back door."

■ ■ ■

A guy is half-Polish and half-Japanese.
He makes calculators that don't work....

□ □ □

Three scientists were given 6 months to live,
and they were told
they could have anything they wanted.
The first scientist was a Frenchman,
and he wanted a beautiful villa on the Riviera
surrounded by gorgeous young girls.
The second scientist was an Englishman,
and he wanted to have tea with the Queen.
The third was a Jewish scientist.
He wanted a second opinion.

My wife is a light eater.
As soon as it's light she starts eating.

Girl overboard....
Father says,
"I'll give half my fortune to save her."
Fellow jumps in and saves girl.
"I'll keep my promise – here's half my fortune."
Guy says,
"I don't want money....
all I want to know is, who pushed me?"

One guy came home and said to his wife,
"Someone showed me an amazing device
that sews buttons right on clothes."
His wife said,
"That's wonderful.
What is it?"
and the guy said,
"A needle and thread."

Lawyer to shoplifting client:
"You shouldn't have taken a hostage."

You know what the Pentagon is.
That's a big building in Washington
that has five sides – on almost every issue!

A Polish lady quit using the pill.
Kept falling out.

What did the Norwegian call his cocktail
of Vodka and Milk of Magnesia? . . .
"A Phillips Screwdriver."

In a little town,
a guy goes to a local barber shop.
It's crowded.
He says, how many ahead of me?
The barber says, five ahead of you.
Man walks out.
Does this for five days in a row.
Finally the barber says to the shoe shine boy
– follow that guy.
See where he goes.
Kid comes back a little later.
Kid says he goes to your house!

I don't mind my wife giving me
all those TV dinners,
but when she starts heating up the leftovers
and calling them re-runs!

It's good to read "Dear Abby" now and then.
What with Russia and Red China
and the H-bomb –
it's wonderful to know
there are still some people
in this world whose biggest worry
is how they should acknowledge
a wedding present.

I understand the Democrats
were gonna run a woman for President,
but she turned it down.
Not enough closets in the White House.

Do you realize it only took six days
to create the world?
Just shows you what can be done
if you don't take a coffee break.

A fellow from New York joins the Israeli army.
After only three days,
he asks for a three day pass.
The colonel asks,
"What are you,
a nut from New York?
You're in the army three days
and already you ask for a pass?
To get a pass
you have to do something sensational."
The next day
the guy drives into camp in an Arab tank.
The amazed colonel asks,
"How did you do it?"
The soldier answers,
"I took one of our tanks
and headed towards Jordan.
I saw one of their tanks coming at me.
The Arab tank put up a white flag.
I put up a white flag. I said to him,
'Do you want to get a three day pass?'
He said yes, so we exchanged tanks."

☆ ☆ ☆

Money talks. . . .
It also stops talk.

□ □ □

My mother-in-law is so nearsighted
she nagged a coat hanger for an hour.

Nowadays
a wedding ring in a maternity ward
is a status symbol.

I just told one of my creditors,
"As long as I owe you, you'll never be broke."

Woman buying fertilizer...
"Is that the only scent it comes in?"

My Doctor made me stop smoking
six months ago....
Now he says I got a tar deficiency.

"How come you live on the third floor
and your apartment is 703?"
"The building settled."

A lady was taking a bath
when the doorbell rang,
so she rushed to the door dripping wet
and asked, "Who is it?"
The answer came, "Blind man."
She figured as long as the man was blind,
there was no need to put on a robe,
so she opened the door, and the man said,
"Where do you want the blinds, lady?"

A man is playing golf.
A leprechaun comes out of the woods
and says to the golfer,
"Would you give up 10 years
of your sex life
if I let you make a hole in one?"
The golfer agrees.
The leprechaun asks,
"Would you give up 10 more years
of your sex life
if I let you make another hole in one?"
The golfer agrees again,
and the leprechaun asks,
"What's your name?"
The happy golfer says, "Father O'Malley."

Guy goes into a bar.
He says, drinks for everybody!
Two drinks for you bartender.
He can't pay, so bartender throws him out.
Comes in next night and does the same thing.
Drinks for everyone.
Two drinks for you bartender.
He can't pay again – this time the bartender
picks up a bat, belts him around and hits him.
Comes in next night, says,
drinks for everybody.
None for you bartender.
You get nasty when you drink.

Two furriers were returning from Miami
and, just for the kick of it,
decided to take a taxi back to New York.
As they were climbing in the cab,
one of them said,
"Let me get in the cab first,
I'm getting out at 72nd Street."

★ ★ ★

Did you watch the Grand P-R-I-X?
I like to spell that word out.

My doctor says
that the arthritis in my finger
is from picking up wet change.

I'm reading a good book...
"The History of Air Conditioning."

The only people who wake up rich
are professional boxers.

Two guys meet, and one says to the other,
"You look bad. What's the matter with you?"
The guy answers,
"I lost three wives in the last three months."
"That's terrible. What happened?"
"My first wife died from eating poisoned
mushrooms."
"What happened to your second wife?"
"She died from eating poisoned mushrooms."
"What happened to your third wife?"
"Fractured skull."
"How come?"
"She wouldn't eat the poisoned mushrooms."

◇ ◇ ◇

Three jewelry salesmen
decide to leave the country;
they want to see what credit
they can get on their jewelry.
One guy gets 30 days credit
and takes off with all the jewelry.
The second gets 60 days credit
and takes off with the jewelry.
The third gets 90 days credit
and does the same.
They pool all the jewelry,
stash it in a coffin and
take it down to Puerto Rico.
They're stopped by a customs inspector
who asks, "Who's in the coffin?"
One fellow says, "That's our brother.
He loved the Puerto Rican people so much
that he asked to be buried over here."
The customs man says,
"That's very nice, but where are the mourners?"
The guy says,
"They'll be along in 30, 60 and 90 days."

☆ ☆ ☆

He plays like Paderewski....
uses both hands.

↓ ➤

35

A 70 year-old man married a girl of 20
and immediately was given advice
by his friends.
One of them said,
"If you want a happy marriage,
you must take in a boarder."
This appealed to the old man,
and a few months later he met his friend
who wanted to know how things
were coming along.
The old man said,
"Things couldn't be better,
and I owe it all to your good advice."
His friend said,
I'm glad to hear it, and how's your wife?"
The old guy said,
"Oh, she's pregnant."
His friend said,
"That's great, and the boarder?"
The old man said,
"Oh, she's pregnant, too!!"

☐ ☐ ☐

If it wasn't for elevators,
most people today
wouldn't know what good music is.

☎

A guy tells his friend,
"My wife is about to have a baby
in the next room.
I'm going to deliver the baby myself."
They hear a scream from the next room,
and the expectant father rushes in.
Five minutes later he comes out and says,
"It's a boy!"
All of a sudden they hear another scream.
The guy rushes in,
comes out five minutes later and says,
"It's twins this time!"
Another scream…he rushes in…
this time he comes out and says,
"Triplets!"
When one more scream is heard
the exhausted father
rushes toward the front door.
His friend asks,
"Where are you going?"
"I want to find out how you
shut the damn thing off!"

▷◁

Won't last long,
they're as compatible as ham and matzos.

‡‡‡

Picture this – a funeral.
Two hearses lead the procession.
Behind them there is a man with a vicious dog.
Behind him follow 100 men in the procession.
A man walking by steps off the curb
and asks the man with the dog,
"What's going on here?"
Pointing to the hearses, the man says,
"That's my wife and mother-in-law.
My dog bit them and killed them."
The man asks, "Can I borrow your dog?"
The widower responds,
"Get in line."

⋈

A guy goes to court for a divorce.
The judge asks,
"Why do you want a divorce?"
He answers,
"Every night, when I come home from work,
instead of my wife being alone,
I find a different guy hiding in our closet."
The judge says,
"And this causes you a lot of unhappiness?"
"It certainly does, Your Honor,
I never have any room to hang up my clothes!"

‡‡‡

A couple is celebrating their 50th anniversary
and visits the old schoolhouse
where they first met and became
childhood sweethearts.
On the drive home
they see a U.S. Treasury truck break open
and a sack of money drop out.
He picks up the sack,
takes it home and hides it in the attic
even though his wife is against the idea.
The next day two FBI agents
show up on their doorstep
and demand that he return the money.
He denies that he has it,
even when his wife tells them he's lying.
One agent says,
"Tell us what happened yesterday."
The man explains,
"My wife and I were coming home
from school. . . ."
One agent says to the other,
"Let's get out of here. This guy is nuts!"

They're not making girls like they used to.
Neither am I.

A man went into a restaurant
and ordered roast beef.
The waiter said,
"Take the chicken pot-pie instead."
The man said,
I don't like chicken pot-pie;
I want roast beef."
The waiter insisted,
"Take the chicken pot-pie."
The man said, "But I don't *want* the pot-pie;
let me talk to the headwaiter."
The headwaiter came over and said,
"What can I do for you?"
The man said,
"I want some roast beef."
The headwaiter said,
"Take the chicken pot-pie instead."
The frustrated man screamed,
"But, damnit, I don't want chicken pot-pie;
I WANT ROAST BEEF.
Let me talk to the manager!"
So the manager came over and said,
"May I help you, Sir?"
The man cried, "Yes!
I asked the waiter for roast beef,
but he insisted
I take the chicken pot-pie instead!
So I asked the headwaiter for some roast beef,

and *he* tried to make me eat the chicken pot-
pie!
Now I'm asking you –
may I *please* have some roast beef???"
The manager turned to the headwaiter
and said,
"Throw this bum out.
He didn't come here to eat;
he just came to argue!"

□ □ □

A priest is sent to Alaska to start a new parish.
He is there for a whole year,
and nobody hears from him.
A bishop goes to investigate.
He asks the priest,
"How do you like it up here in Alaska?"
The priest says, "If it weren't for my rosary
and two martinis a day, you could keep Alaska.
Bishop, would you like a martini?"
The bishop nods, and the priest hollers,
"Rosary, get the bishop a martini!"

☎

They were such a beautiful couple. . . .
They even stood on their own wedding cake.

☆ ☆ ☆

On top of a hill on the Israeli border
is an Israeli guard.
On a cliff facing him is an Arab guard.
The Israeli guard is shouting out,
"Thirteen, thirteen, thirteen.…"
Finally the annoyed Arab guard
shouts out to him,
"What are you hollering out
thirteen all the time for?
What does it mean?"
The Israeli guard says,
"Step over here, and I'll show you."
The Arab takes a step forward
and falls off the cliff.
The Israeli guard watches,
then starts to holler,
"Fourteen, fourteen, fourteen.…"

★ ★ ★

When I met Walter Pigeon
I got real nervous and said,
"Mr. Privilege, this certainly is a pigeon."

◊ ◊ ◊

Toast: He who loves and runs away,
lives to love another day.

A guy comes home from work,
gets in the door and hollers,
"Ethel! There is a rumor around
that you are leaving me."
He hollers out,
"Ethel!...(louder)
Ethel!...(louder) ETHEL!"

‡‡‡

Rip Van Winkle woke up twenty years later.
His wife shook him.
Rip says, "Five minutes more, Mom!"

†††

I don't know what to do with my wife.
Yesterday she was cleaning the attic
and found a case of seventeen year old Scotch.
So she threw it out.
Figured it was stale.

☛↓

A drunk falls down an empty elevator shaft.
He's laying there bleeding.
He says,
"I said up!"

☚☛

The Russians were anxious to contact
one of their spies over here
but had no way of conveying the code
without someone intercepting,
so they sent a submarine off our shore
and tried to contact him by telephone.
They found two Goldbergs
in the town he lived in
so they waited until after midnight
and phoned one of them.
The code was,
"Roses are red, Violets are blue,
America, America, I...Love...You!"
They got the first man on the phone
and repeated the code,
"Roses are red, Violets are blue,
America, America, I...Love...You!"
The first man said,
"Oh, you got the wrong Goldberg.
I'm Goldberg the tailor.
You want Goldberg the spy.
He lives across the street!"

◊ ◊ ◊

Old folks held an Olympiad...
most popular event was long distance dialing.

Two girls win a contest.
They get a free trip to Africa.
They each get a tent for themselves.
In the middle of the night
a gorilla goes into one of the tents
and rapes one of the girls.
This happens every night in the week.
She's ashamed to tell her girl friend,
so she doesn't say anything.
They get back to New York,
then she tells her girl friend what happened.
The girl friend says,
"Well it could happen to anyone.
Why are you so depressed?"
The girl replies,
"He don't call, he don't write...."

□ □ □

Drunk falls down and says,
"I think there is too much gravity around here."

Bad day
when you hear on the airplane intercom...
"This is your captain speaking,
they will never take me alive."

James Watt's idea of a wildlife refuge
is a parking lot without stress.

Trust everybody...
but it doesn't hurt to cut the cards.

My luck...
I was waiting at the airport
when my ship came in.

A guy is brought in front of a judge
for speeding. The judge says,
"You have been accused
of going 80 miles an hour.
What do have to say for yourself?"
The guy says,
"Judge, I wasn't going 80 miles an hour.
I wasn't going 70 miles an hour.
I wasn't going 60 miles an hour.
I wasn't going 40 miles an hour...."
The judge says,
"Give this guy a ticket
before he backs into somebody."

My shrink doesn't have a couch...
he uses a sleeping bag.

There was a fellow who made it his business
to crash every party.
No matter what it was,
he was there,
eating,
drinking
and carrying on.
One day someone approached him at an affair
and said,
"Are you a friend of the bride and groom?"
And he said, "Am I?
Why I knew the bride
when she was just a little tot
this high."
And the guy said,
"Well, get the hell outta here,
this is a Bar Mitzvah!"

‡‡‡

If Christian Scientists were more scientific
and doctors were more Christian,
all you'd need would be a good nurse.

The trouble with girls today
is that all they can do is thaw food.
Why can't they open cans
like their mothers did?

‡‡‡

Income tax:
That's the government's version
of instant poverty.

Y

There is a Polish guy
who hates Polish jokes about
Polish people being stupid.
He studies English for two years
to try and better himself.
After two years he goes into a store
and says in perfect English,
"I would like to have
a half pound of caviar, please.
I would also like some Scotch salmon."
The salesman says, "You're Polish, aren't you?"
The Polish guy is crushed and asks,
"How did you know?"
The salesman says,
"You're in a hardware store."

☎

Want to have some fun?
Walk into an antique shop and say,
"What's new?"

For Christmas I gave my kid a chemistry set,
and now I'm getting worried.
The last time I tried to spank him,
he held up a vial and yelled:
"Lay one finger on me,
and we'll all go up together!"

A new salesman in one of those
new-fashioned drug stores
that carry thousands of items
sold $3000 worth
of fishing equipment to a customer.
Amazed, the boss asks,
"How did you manage to sell $3000 worth of
equipment on your first day on the job?"
The salesman answers,
"A man came in and asked
for a box of Tampax for his wife,
so I said to him,
'While you're not doing anything,
why don't you go fishing?'"

An Englishman comes home,
finds his wife in bed with three men.
Do you know what the Englishman said?
He said, "Hello, hello, hello!"
His wife said, "Don't you talk to me?"

☛ ↓

A dentist opened an office in a small town
and to establish good will
was very generous
with some of the clergy in town.
One day a priest came to have a tooth pulled,
but the dentist wouldn't charge him for it,
so the priest sent him some rosary beads
as a gift.
Another day a minister came
for some treatment,
and again the dentist wouldn't charge him,
so the minister sent the dentist a Bible
for a gift.
The following week a rabbi came
for some treatment,
and again the dentist refused
to accept any money.
You know what the Rabbi sent him?
Another rabbi.

↓ ☚

A coach of a football team
where they had a lot of racial problems said,
"Look, there's no more black guys
and no more white guys on this team.
From now on everybody is one color – green."
They got out on the playing field,
and he gave orders,
"All right,
all the light green guys on this side,
and all the dark green ones on that side."

A doctor was discussing medical problems
with a retired executive's wife
who was complaining that her husband
didn't have as much sexual drive
as he had had on their honeymoon.
The doctor asked,
"How old are you?"
She said,
"I'm 72."
"And what is your husband's age?"
"He's 86."
Then the doctor asked,
"When did you first notice these symptoms?"
The old lady said,
"First last night and again this morning!"

A guy is stopping at
the Fountainbleu Hotel in Miami.
He is being paged over the phone.
"Mr. Schwartz, your suite is ready."
He says, "What suite?
I want the whole floor to myself.
I'm Jay Schwartz from New York!"
At noon he gets a call.
"Mr. Schwartz, your table in the dining room
is ready for lunch." He says, "What table?
I want the whole dining room to myself.
I'm Jay Schwartz from New York –
don't forget it!"
After lunch he goes out to the cabana.
He is lying there, enjoying the sun,
and he says to himself,
" I wish I could afford all this!"

He not only knows the golden oldies –
he dates them!

□ □ □

The reason she says we don't get along
is that she is a Scorpio,
and I'm a librarian.

A guy who is contemplating marriage
tells the girl,
"Before we get serious
I want you to know that I'm an avid golfer.
I play golf every minute of my life that I can.
For instance, if you were hit by a car, and
an ambulance was on its way to pick you up,
and I had an appointment to play golf,
I would keep my golf date."
She says, "I want you to know I'm a hooker."
He says,
"Maybe you're not holding the club right."

Two hoity-toity women from the Bronx
were lying under an umbrella at Miami Beach
when one asked the other,
"What did you do to your hair?
The color...
the texture...
it looks like a wig."
And her friend said,
"It *is* a wig!"
And the first one said,
"Really?
You know, you could never tell."

There is a stuttering jeweler
who runs a little shop.
A customer rushes in and says,
"Take this watch and have it cleaned.
Put in a new movement,
and put on a new strap.
I'll be back in twenty minutes."
As the man is about to rush out,
the jeweler says,
"C-c-c-c...come in!"

It must be wonderful to be a doctor.
In what other job could you ask a girl
to take her clothes off,
look her over at your leisure,
and then send a bill to her husband?

A girl was knocking at my door all night long –
I finally had to let her out of my room.

The hardest thing for him after the divorce
was learning to talk again.

The president of Macy's
was awakened one morning about 3 a.m.,
and when he answered the phone
some man said,
"Good morning, this is Jim O'Leary.
You don't know me, but I bought a coffee table
at your store two weeks ago,
and I just wanna tell you
how much I like the table."
The president said,
"Well, that's fine,
but why did you have to call me
in the middle of the night to tell me that?"
The guy said,
"Because your damn truck just delivered it!"

There's this guy
who sits in front of the television all weekend.
Day and night, he watches football games.
His wife takes all her clothes off,
puts her raincoat on
and runs back and forth
in front of the television set.
She says,
"Either play me or trade me."

A hunter is lost in the woods –
he comes upon a monastery.
Outside the monastery the friars in their habits
and the monks are working.
He walks into the monastery,
he tells them that he's lost and is hungry.
They invite him to have dinner.
They served him fish and chips.
He loves the fish. He says,
"I'd like to meet the man who made the fish."
They bring the man out of the kitchen.
He says, "Are you the fish friar?"
The man says, "No, I'm the chip monk."

Isn't it amazing the way carts
have taken the place of caddies
on the golf course?
Let's face it –
they have three big advantages:
they don't cost,
they don't criticize
and they don't count!

Cheap?...His hearing aid is on a party line.

A little French boy came home from the zoo.
His father asked, "Did you enjoy the zoo?"
The boy nodded and answered,
"Yes, Papa. Mama showed me the elephant.
I asked her, 'What is that thing hanging down
in the back of the elephant?'
She said, 'That is the tail.'
Then I asked her what was that thing hanging
down in front of the elephant,
and she said, 'That is the trunk.'
Then I asked her
what is that other thing hanging down,
and she said, 'That is nothing.'"
The father says to the boy,
"Ahhh, my son, your mother has been spoiled."

Some men are born great,
and some men
have greatness thrust upon them...
like Dolly Parton's husband.

In Las Vegas, a guy running up and down
putting money in parking meters.
He says, "I love this outdoor gambling!"

This kid gets out of college,
and his father greets him with open arms.
"Partner, my partner.
Now you'll come into my business
as an equal partner.
You'll start at the bottom as a dishwasher
and learn the business."
The kid says,
"Me? Be a dishwasher?
And I'm your partner?"
The father says,
"Okay, okay, you'll be a waiter
and meet all our customers."
The kid says,
"Me? Be a lowly waiter? Your partner?"
The father says,
"Okay, okay, Mr. Bigshot,
so what do you want to do?"
The kid says,
"Pop, I don't like the way you're talking to me.
I think you ought to buy me out!"

■ ■ ■

Would you believe it,
I used to play at Carnegie Hall –
till the cops chased me away.

✀

A guy says to a doctor,
"I'm having trouble with my love life at home."
The doctor says,
"Take off 20 pounds
and run 10 miles a day
for two weeks."
Two weeks later,
the guy calls the doctor,
"Doctor, I took off 20 pounds,
and I've been running 10 miles a day."
The doctor asks,
"How is your love life now?"
"I don't know,
I'm 140 miles away!"

In the State of Israel they were holding
ceremonies for the Unknown Soldier,
when one of the guests noticed the name
of Morris Liebowitz on the tomb.
He asked the commanding officer,
"If this is the tomb of the Unknown Soldier,
why is his name on the tomb?"
The officer said,
"As a *soldier* he was unknown,
but as a *furrier* he was the best!"

◊ ◇ ◊

When Colonel John Glenn
made the famous space trip
I phoned my mother, and I said,
"Mom, did you hear the news
about Colonel Glenn?"
She said, "What news? Who's Glenn?"
I said,
"Mom, he's the famous astronaut
who went around the world three times!"
She said,
"Well,
when you got money, you can travel!"

It's just wonderful,
the generosity of Americans.
I know one outfit
that's already collected $3,000,000 —
and they don't even have a disease yet!

Believe me,
it's getting to the point
where you need more brains
to make out the income tax forms
than to make the income.

☆ ☆ ☆

At our country club,
one of the members dropped dead.
Nobody wanted to tell his wife,
so the doctor said he'd do it.
He called and said,
"Mrs. Cohen, your husband, Sam,
lost $500 playing cards at the club."
The wife yelled,
"He should drop dead."
The doctor said,
"He did."

Genoa Airlines merged with Alitalia...
Now it's called Genitalia.

☆ ☆ ☆

In Hollywood they have community property.
A couple gets divorced,
she gets the Jaguar,
he gets the radiator ornament.

St. Patrick's has a drive-in confessional.
You toot and tell.

† † †

Quasimodo was showing his young apprentice
how to ring the churchbell.
He explained,
"You push the bell and then get out of the way,
or it hits you in the kisser."
Sure enough the kid pushes the bell
and forgets to get out of the way.
It hits him
and knocks him off the church steeple.
Quasimodo runs downstairs
and looks at the kid.
A cop asks if he knows the victim,
and Quasimodo answers,
"His face doesn't ring a bell."
His brother takes over
and also falls from the belfry.
When Quasimodo is questioned he says,
"He's a dead ringer for his brother!"

□ □ □

I guess you heard about the fella
who invented an electric car.
For three dollars worth of electricity
you can drive it from Los Angeles to New York.
There's only one hitch –
a $5,000 extension cord!

A garment manufacturer
came back from Rome
and was telling his partner
about the famous fountain.
His partner said,
"And did you throw a coin in the fountain
for good luck?"
And he said,
"I didn't have any change,
so I threw in a check!"

My mother was 88 years old.
She never used glasses.
Drank right out of the bottle!

A little old lady goes into court
to get a divorce.
The judge asks,
"How old are you?"
"Sixty."
"How long have you been married?"
"Forty years."
"What do you want a divorce for?"
"Ah, enough is enough!"

A guy calls his home and says to the maid,
"Where's my wife?"
The maid answers, "Your wife is in the bedroom
with your best friend."
Furious, the man says,
"Okay, Maria, go to the drawer,
get my gun out and shoot the both of them!"
Two gun shots ring out,
then she returns to the phone.
"Maria, what did you do with the gun?"
She answers, "I threw it in the pool."
He says, "What pool? We don't have a pool.
Isn't this TR4-5355?"

■ ■ ■

A guy swallows a ping pong ball.
The doctor cuts him in four places.
The guy says, "Hey, what's the idea,
cutting me in four places?"
The doctor says,
"That's the way the ball bounces!"

✂

To the man who robbed
the First National Bank yesterday:
Your photos are ready.

‡‡‡

A couple won a contest.
First prize is a week
at the Watergate Hotel in Washington.
When they get to their suite,
the bride is acting very nervous.
"What's wrong, darling?" the husband asks.
She says, "This is the Watergate Hotel.
Maybe this place is still being bugged.
He looks behind the curtains,
behind the shade,
picks up the carpet
and spots a disk with four screws.
He removes the screws and the disk
and puts them away.
The next morning
the manager knocks on the door.
"Good morning, Mr. and Mrs. Welzer.
How do you like the suite?"
The man answers, "Beautiful!"
The manager looks nervous.
"How did you like the dinner,
the caviar and the champagne we sent you?"
The man answers, "Wonderful, but why are you
keep asking me so many questions?"
The manager says,
"The couple in the room below complained
the chandelier fell on them!"

She's going to have her face capped.

A penny-pinching penguin,
asked by his son to explain the difference
between valor and discretion, replied,
"Valor, my boy,
is dining in a high-class restaurant
and not tipping the waiter.
Discretion is eating
at another restaurant next time!"

◊ ◇ ◊

This guy says to a waiter,
"How come you serve pizza
in a Chinese restaurant?"
The waiter says,
"We have to... it's a Jewish neighborhood!"

★ ★ ★

Wife to husband –
"How come you don't play gin rummy
with Sol Schwartz anymore?"
"Would you play with anyone who cheats?"
"Certainly not!"
"Well, neither will he!"

It's reassuring to see that colleges
are putting the emphasis on education again.
One school has gotten so strict,
it won't even give a football player his letter,
unless he can tell which one it is.

†††

A lush was hauled into court for being drunk
and disorderly.
When the judge saw him he said,
"Drunk again, eh?"
And the lush said,
"Man's inhumanity to man
makes thousands mourn.
I am not so debased as Poe,
so profligate as Byron,
so ungrateful as Keats,
so intemperate as Burns,
so demented as Tennyson,
so vulgar as Shakespeare...."
The judge interrupted him and said,
"That's enough of that.
Seven days in the slammer,
and, Officer, take down those names
he mentioned and round 'em all up.
They're as bad as he is!"

A man goes down to the ship company –
he wants to know the cheapest trip
he can get to Bermuda.
The guy says,
"We can give you a suite for $2,500."
"No, that's too expensive."
"Well, we have a room for $500."
He says, "That's too expensive,
what is the cheapest trip you have?"
'We have one trip where you get in a boat
with 12 guys, and you row across."

Internal Revenue Service –
The world's most successful
mail-order business.

Remember when Charge!
meant the Light Brigade,
not the Diner's Club?

It's one of those British science-fiction pictures.
You can tell it's British
because the Martians all carry umbrellas!

★ ★ ★

A rugged Texan,
dripping with oil and Cadillacs,
walked into an exclusive art gallery
in New York with his nagging wife.
In fifteen minutes flat the Texan bought
six Picassos,
three Renoirs,
ten Cezannes
and thirty Utrillos.
He then turned to his wife
and with a sigh of relief said,
"There, honey child,
that takes care of the Christmas cards.
Now let's get started on the serious shopping."

One man asked another,
"What do you think
of this Watergate scandal?"
The other man, who stuttered, said,
"They oughta...oughta...oughta take...
take...take all...all...all those guys
and throw...throw them out of the...the...
the...government and start over."
The other guy said,
"That's easy for you to say!"

I saw a funny thing in Miami today.
I saw a woman in a cloth coat.

A woman went into the office of a cemetery
and told the manager that she couldn't find
her husband's grave.
She said, "There's something wrong here.
I know this is where he's buried!"
The manager said, "What's his name?"
And she said, "Sam Shapiro."
He looked through the card index
and finally said,
"Sam Shapiro we haven't got;
we got a Sarah Shapiro."
And she said, "That's him!
Everything's in my name!"

☎

I just finished filling out my income tax form.
Who said you can't get wounded by a blank?

I once wanted to become an atheist,
but I gave it up –
they have no holidays.

I know a woman who went to a clinic
where they had about eight doctors.
After fifteen minutes in one doctor's office
she ran screaming down the hall.
Another doctor, who finally got the story
out of her and calmed her down,
called the first doctor.
"What's the idea of telling Miss Jones
she's pregnant when she's not?
You scared her to death!"
"I know," the first doctor said,
"but I sure cured her hiccups, didn't I?"

★ ★ ★

A Bohemian decided to drive to Omaha
to see his cousin.
About 20 miles from his destination,
he saw a sign, "BEAR LEFT."
So he turned around and went back home.

He spends money like water...
drip, drip, drip, drip....

Best diet is to never eat on an empty stomach.

Krebs was killed in an accident,
and Silverman was sent to break the news
to his wife.
"Be careful how you tell her,"
advised a friend.
"She's a very delicate woman!"
He knocked on the door, and she came out.
"Pardon me,
are you the widow Krebs?"
"Certainly not."
"You wanna bet?"

A fellow joined the army
and was given one of the routine uniforms.
He immediately went to one of those
problem-solver professors and said,
"Professor, I just joined the army,
and they gave me this uniform.
You see that the coat is the right length;
the sleeves and pants are the right length;
the hat fits me perfectly;
and my shoes are the right size.
So my problem is this:
am I deformed?"

In a congregation in a hillbilly county,
the deacon was taking an inventory
of the congregation.
He asked the married men to stand up.
They got up and sat down.
Then he asked for the married women
to stand up,
which they did and sat down.
Then he asked for the single men
and the single women to stand up;
they did and sat down.
Then he cried,
"Will the virgins
of the congregation stand up?"
Up got a fat dame with a tiny baby in her arms.
The deacon yelled,
"I said the virgins."
To which she replied,
"Listen, dope.
How do you expect a two-month-old baby
to stand up by herself?"

□ □ □

This cancer scare is getting so bad,
Indians are smoking filtered peace pipes.

† † †

73

A Polish girl walks into a bar
with a duck under her arm.
Bartender: "You can't come in here with a pig."
Girl: "This ain't a pig…it's a duck."
Bartender: "I wasn't talking to you…!
I was talking to the duck."

☎

As the honorable Senator from Texas
once put it:
"When those Eskimos convinced Congress
to make Alaska the 49th state
the American people got
the biggest snow job in history!"

✂

Woman: Oh, my goodness….
my husband is driving in the driveway!
Norwegian: I better get outta here.
Vhere is your back door?
Woman: We don't have a back door.
Norwegian: Vell, where vould you like vun?

▷◦◁

My doctor is an eye, ear, nose
and throat and wallet specialist!

★ ★ ★

A sign saying, "Jesus saves."
Underneath it somebody wrote,
"Moses invests."

Rachel: "I was to Doctor Horowitz today...
and what a thrill!
He said he had never seen such a perfect body."
Max: "What did he say about your fat ass?"
Rachel: "Funny thing,
he didn't even mention you."

Two friends meet.
One says, "You look bad,
what's the matter with you?"
He says, "I was in London
where there is a six-hour difference in time,
and I couldn't sleep, and my timing is off.
I sit down to eat, I get sleepy.
I go to bed, I get hungry!"

How do you identify a Polish intellectual?
When you see one
not moving his lips while reading.

Sam Goldberg just got back
from a trip to Paris,
and he was telling his friend,
"What a place!
But I wish I saw it 50 years ago."
And his friend said,
"You mean when Paris was really Paris?"
And Goldberg said,
"No, when Goldberg was really Goldberg!"

◆◆◆

Woman: I was just raped by a Pole.
Policeman: How do you know he was Polish?
Woman: I had to show him how.

☞↓

They taught a dumb guy
how to run a helicopter.
It's up 800 feet.
All of a sudden it falls to the ground.
I said to him, "What happened?"
He says, "It got chilly up there
so I turned off the fan."

‡‡‡

His errogenous zone is the western hemisphere.

Why don't Polish mothers
nurse their babies? . . .
Because it is so painful
when they boil the nipples.

In San Francisco
they have a new dumb mime group.
They talk!

■ ■ ■

There's a new Norwegian insurance policy.
It's called "My Fault Insurance."

I love the Italian people.
During World War II
an Italian girl saved my life.
She hid me in her cellar.
It was on Mulberry Street!

A hold-up man
walks into a Chinese restaurant and says,
"Give me all your cash."
The Chinaman asks, "To take out?"

HENNY YOUNGMAN

My wife Sadie just had plastic surgery –
I cut up her credit cards.

↓ ☞

A Swede had trouble putting
"Happy birthday" on a cake.
His main problem was getting
the cake in the typewriter.

† † †

Goldberg was walking through
the garment district
when he spotted an old friend.
He ran up, slapped him on the back and yelled,
"Abe Lefkowitz! Am I glad to see *you*?
What's happened to you?
Last time I saw you, you were short and fat,
now you're tall and thin…
you were sick, maybe?"
The second man said, "I'm sorry, Mister,
but my name ain't Abe Lefkowitz."
Goldberg says, "Changed your name too, huh?"

☐ ☐ ☐

Two dumb guys with burnt faces.
They were bobbing for French fries!

A teacher taking over a new class
asked a little boy his name.
"Julie," he replied.
"Not Julie," she said.
"You shouldn't use contractions.
Your name is Julius."
Turning to the next boy, she asked,
"And what is your name?"
"Billious," he replied.

Did you hear about the Norwegian
who had his bathroom carpeted?
He liked it so well that he had it carpeted
all the way to the house.

☆ ☆ ☆

A Pole appeared with five other men
in a rape case police line-up.
As the girl entered the room, the Pole blurted,
"Yep...that's her!"

There was a dumb terrorist
sent to blow up a car.
He burnt his lips on the exhaust pipe!

◆◆◆

Man takes his boss home for dinner.
A woman lets them in.
Boss says, "Is that your wife?"
He says, "Would I hire a maid that ugly?"

Sandy McTavish, a true and thrifty Scotsman,
in a burst of generosity
decided to give his wife a mink outfit
for her birthday.
A trap and a rifle.

Two Jewish women in the building –
one says to the other,
"Did you hear there is a rapist in the building?"
She says, "Yes, I know.
I already gave."

Patrick the Irishman
let it be known around the neighborhood
that he had become a diamond cutter.
Later the neighbors found out
that he mowed grass at the ball park.

A Norwegian, an Irishman and a German
were sentenced to be electrocuted.
First, the Irishman was strapped in the chair,
and the switch was pushed.
Nothing happened, so the Irishman was freed.
Same thing happened to the German.
As the Norwegian was led
into the execution room,
the prison guard remarked,
"Sure has been a lucky day for those two guys."
Said the Norwegian, "Vell, I should say so,
becoss I can see the plug
has come out of the socket under the chair."

†††

Some guy bought 1000 garbarge trucks.
He's selling them to the Polish police
as condominiums with escalators!

↓ 🔨

A Norwegian decided to take up hunting.
So, off into the woods he went. . . .
when suddenly a beautiful blonde appeared.
"Are you game?" asked the Norsky.
"I certainly am," purred the blonde.
So he shot her.

✂

Banker is swimming in the water.
A shark comes towards him and veers away.
Professional courtesy.

I just had a wonderful dream.
I dreamed the Joneses
were trying to keep up with me!

A Jewish woman in the Bronx
recently caused quite a commotion
by revealing the contents of her will.
First, she stipulated that she be cremated.
Then, she asked that her ashes
be spread over Bloomingdale's
so she'd be assured of having her daughter
visit her at least twice a week.

When we were married 50 years
we went back to the same hotel
where we got married,
had the same suite of rooms,
only this time
I went into the bathroom and cried!

April 15th...
the day when millions of Americans
realize they've got an extra person
on their payroll –
Uncle Sam!

Did you ever see
one of those Italian movies?...
like *Bread, Love and Pizza* or
Bread, Love and Mozzarella?

I think there's a lot more truthfulness
in advertising than there used to be.
Two weeks ago I bought
one of those collapsible swimming pools
for the kids.
This morning it did.

†††

When a guy says he's fixed for life,
you don't know whether
he's talking about a pension
or a vasectomy.

83

An elderly couple went to a doctor.
The man said, "We want to know
if we're making love properly.
Will you look at us?"
The doctor said, "Go ahead."
So they made love.
The doctor said, "You're making love perfectly.
That will be $10.00."
They came back six weeks in a row
and did the same thing.
On the seventh visit the doctor said,
"What are you coming here like this for –
I told you you're making love properly."
The man said, "She can't come to my house.
I can't go to her house.
You charge us $10.00,
the motel costs us $20.00,
and we get $8.00 back from Medicare."

■ ■ ■

The bookies were coming out
of a church service.
One was rapping the other on the head
and saying,
"How many times have I told you –
it's Hallalujah, not Hialeah!"

There is a man stretched out on his back
across four seats in a theater.
An usher comes down and says,
"Mister, you will have to get out
of those four seats.
You are only entitled to one seat."
The man just grunts and doesn't move.
The manager comes down and says to the man,
"Mister, you'll have to get up.
All you're entitled to is one seat."
The man grunts and doesn't move.
Finally a policeman is called in.
He walks down the aisle and says to the man
who is still lying on the four seats,
"Get out of those seats!"
The man grunts.
The policeman says,
"Okay, wise guy, where are you from?"
The man says, "The balcony!"

↓ ▬

I know one football player
who's been in college for 13 years,
it's kind of a sad story.
He can run, and he can kick –
but he can't pass.

☐ ☐ ☐

Saved a girl from being raped.
I controlled myself.

Let's face it,
the American businessman is in a tight spot.
Whenever he comes up with something new,
The Russians invent it a month later,
and the Japanese make it cheaper!

A prisoner is going to the electric chair.
The warden says,
"You can have anything you want
for your last meal."
The prisoner says,
"I want strawberries."
The warden says,
"Strawberries won't be in season
for six months."
The prisoner says,
"I'll wait."

I miss my wife's cooking –
as often as I can.

Have you noticed
that most people who give up smoking
substitute something for it?
Irritability!

▷∘◁

A woman called another woman on the phone
and asked her how she was feeling.
The other woman said, "Terrible!
My head's splitting,
and my back and legs are killing me,
and the house is a mess,
and the children are driving me crazy!"
The caller said,
"Listen, go and lie down.
I'll come right over and cook lunch for you,
and I'll clean the house and watch the children
while you get some rest.
By the way,
how's your husband, Sam."
The woman said,
"Sam? I got no husband Sam."
The first woman said,
"My goodness,
I must have dialed the wrong number. . . ."
The complaining woman asked,
Does this mean that you're not coming over?"

☛ ↓

A fire broke out
in an apartment house one night,
and all the tenants rushed out into the street
carrying their prized possessions.
One old man was carrying
a large covered bird-cage.
The woman who lived next door to him
asked him what he had in the cage,
and he said, "My pet rooster."
The woman fainted.
When they brought her to, she said,
"I'm sorry I fainted,
but I've been under treatment for the past year
by a psychiatrist because I kept hearing a
rooster crowing!"

A woman used to go to a doctor
to ask if she could have children.
Now she asks the landlord.

Abe Lincoln,
after a five day drunk,
woke up and said,
"I freed who?"

Two business partners,
Levine and Rappaport,
decided to change their names.
First Levine changed his name to Godfrey,
and later on his partner took the same name.
One day someone called
and told the receptionist,
"I'd like to talk to Mr. Godfrey."
And she said,
"Which one,
Levine or Rappaport?"

□ □ □

My best friend ran away with my wife,
and, let me tell you,
I miss him.

†††

Doctor's wife:
"John, why did you cut
the back part
of the book I bought you?"
Doctor:
"Oh dear,
it was marked 'appendix,'
and I removed it."

†††

A couple married 25 years is celebrating
their silver wedding anniversary.
The wife splurges –
Waldorf room... Cugat band...
caviar... champagne...
silver gifts for all the guests.
The husband bemoans his fate.
His lawyer stops and asks,
"Why the gloom, Sam?
This is a big, happy occasion."
Sam says,
"Remember I came to you
when I was 5 years married,
and asked you what would happen
if I stabbed my wife,
and you said I would get 20 years?
Well, tonight I would be a free man!"

◆◆◆

Personally, I detest gambling.
I'm so set against gambling,
I'll bet 2 to 1 they'll never legalize it.

Why are my questions always more interesting
than your answers?

Have you tried vodka and carrot juice?
You get drunk just as fast,
but your eyesight gets better.

"I understand your husband drowned
and left you two million dollars.
Can you imagine two million dollars,
and he couldn't even read or write?"
She said,
Yeah...and he couldn't swim either."

☆ ☆ ☆

A man was driving his car with his wife
in the back seat
when it got stalled on a railroad track
with a train coming head on.
His wife began to scream,
"Go on, keep going,
there's a train coming!"
And her husband said,
"Look! You've been driving
from the back seat all day.
Well, I've got MY end across,
now you see what YOU can do
with YOUR END!"

In one of the Catskill hotels
there was a Chinese waiter
who spoke fluent Jewish.
As he'd take the orders
he would yell them back to the kitchen
in Jewish.
One of the guests asked the boss,
"Where did you ever get a Chinese waiter
who speaks Jewish?"
And the boss said,
"Shhh,
he thinks we're teaching him English!"

▷◁

The other day a policeman stopped a man going
the wrong way on a one-way street,
"Didn't you see the arrow?"
"Arrow?
Honest officer,
I didn't even see the Indians."

☆ ☆ ☆

Have you noticed how many more twins
are being born than ever before?
I think the kids are getting afraid
to come into the world alone.

↓ 🖐

In Miami Beach there is a grandmother
sitting at the beach.
She's supposed
to be watching her grandson in the water.
She turns her head away to talk to somebody.
All of a sudden a storm comes along
and washes the little boy way out in the ocean.
They call the lifeguards,
the police,
the coast guard,
a helicopter.
They finally get the boy ashore.
They pump him out.
The boy starts to breathe again.
The grandmother says,
"He had a hat!"

Two Israelis are about to be shot by six Arabs.
One Israeli says to the other one,
"I think I'm going to ask for a blindfold."
The other says,
"Sam, don't make trouble."

Rich?...He takes cabs to drive-in movies.

A man can't find a lawyer,
so he picks up the yellow pages
and picks out a law firm –
Schwartz, Schwartz, Schwartz, and Schwartz.
He calls up and says,
Is Mr. Schwartz there?"
A guy says,
"No, he's out playing golf."
He says,
"All right, then let me talk to Mr. Schwartz."
He says,
"He's not with the firm anymore; he's retired."
"Okay, then let me talk to Mr. Schwartz."
"Oh, he's away in Detroit,
won't be back for a month."
Okay, then let me talk to Mr. Schwartz.
He says,
"Speaking!"

☆ ☆ ☆

Things were rough when I was a baby.
No talcum powder.

▷◁

President Reagan met my wife.
He declared my home a disaster area.

✄

A man has been smoking cigarettes
for 20 years.
He takes one puff from a cigarette,
throws it down and steps on it.
He does this all day long.
What do you think this man has today?
Cancer of the shoe.

▷◁

An absent-minded maestro was rushing up
Broadway on his way to a rehearsal when a
stranger stopped him and said,
"Pardon me, can you tell me how to get to
Carnegie Hall?"
And the maestro said,
"PRACTICE, PRACTICE!"

☛↓

A guy in the clothing business goes to Italy
and by luck gets an audience with the Pope.
He calls his partner in New York and says,
"What do you think?
I had an audience with the Pope!"
The partner says, "Really?
What kind of a guy is the Pope?"
His partner says, "He's a regular 38."

A woman was getting fed up with her husband,
who was the worst of golf addicts.
She cried to him one morning,
"We are having company for dinner tonight,
and I want you home from your golf game
sharply at 5 p.m."
He promised he would be home on time.
He walked in at 9 p.m.
His wife was now in a rage.
She cried,
"You promised to be home at five o'clock;
you lied to me!"
"Listen. Hear me out.
You know James Coddingtone.
Right in the middle of the golf game
he dropped with a heart attack.
Between dragging the body and hitting the ball
and dragging the body
and hitting the ball...."

I have a brother-in-law so smart
that during the garbage strike,
do you know how he got rid of it?
Gift wrapped it, put it in the back of his car,
and they stole it.

◊ ◇ ◊

For eight days and nights,
Schlossberg the suit maker was unable to sleep.
No medicine took effect, and in desperation
the Schlossberg family brought in
a famous hypnotist.
The hypnotist stared at Schlossberg
and chanted,
"You are asleep, Mr. Schlossberg.
The shadows are closing about you.
Soft music is lulling you into a state
of lovely relaxation.
You are asleep! You are asleep!"
"You're a miracle worker,"
sobbed the grateful son.
He gave the hypnotist a big bonus,
and the man left in triumph.
As the outside door closed,
Schlossberg opened one eye.
"Say," he demanded, "is that idiot gone yet?"

WINDOW SIGN IN KORNFELD'S
CLOTHING STORE
USE OUR EASY CREDIT PLAN:
100 PERCENT DOWN
NOTHING TO PAY EACH MONTH!

■ ■ ■

A young playboy went to Miami
but found himself short of cash.
When he found out that his hotel
was charging $50 a day for room,
meals and golf privileges,
he went across the street
to an equally elegant hotel
where the rates were only $10 a day.
The next morning he went down
to the hotel's golf course
and asked the pro to sell him
a couple of golf balls.
The pro said,
"Sure. That will be $25 apiece."
The playboy yelled, "What?
Twenty-five dollars apiece for golf balls?
Why in that hotel across the street
they only charge $1 a ball!"
And the golf pro said, "Sure.
Over there they get you by the ROOMS!"

☎

Camp Hiawatha, Camp Senecca,
that's where the Jewish kids
go for the summer.
Camp Ginsberg is where the Indian kids go.

‡‡‡

A movie producer advertised for a Texan,
6 feet tall, 200 pounds.
One morning about 3 o'clock
he got a phone call in answer to the ad
from a fellow who spoke with a Jewish accent.
The producer said,
"You don't sound like a Texan."
And the fellow said,
"That's right, I ain't, I'm from New York."
The producer said,
"Are you six feet tall,
and do you weigh 200 pounds?"
And the fellow said,
"No, I'm 5 feet 5, and I weight 110 pounds."
The producer was furious as he yelled,
"Then what the hell are you phoning me for
at 3 o'clock in the morning?"
And the Jewish feller said,
"I just called to tell you,
ON ME YOU SHOULDN'T DEPEND!"

☛↓

Famous inventions:
The Poles invented the toilet seat.
Twenty years later,
the Italians invented the hole in it.

‡‡‡

Indian girl marries Jewish boy.
They have to give their new son a name
to please both sides of the family.
They named him "Whitefish."

⋈

Despite warnings from his guide,
an American skiing in Switzerland
got separated from his group
and fell – uninjured –
into a deep crevasse.
Several hours later,
a rescue party found the yawning pit,
and, to reassure the stranded skier,
shouted down to him,
"We're from the Red Cross."
"Sorry,"
the imperturbable American echoed back,
"I already gave at the office!"

‡‡‡

A man bragging about his new hearing aid.
"It's the best I've ever had.
It costs $2,500."
His friend asked, "What kind is it?"
He said, "Half past four!"

☛↓

A woman never gets taken anywhere
by her husband.
She says, "What would it take
for you to go on a second honeymoon?"
He says, "A second wife."

I know a guy that was so active,
that five years after he died,
his self-winding watch was still running.

Whistler's mother was doing a handstand.
Her son asked, "What's the matter, Ma,
you off your rocker?"

A rich old garment manufacturer died,
and his family met in the lawyer's office
for the reading of his will.
He left $300,000 to his wife,
$100,000 to his brothers
and $10,000 each to his sisters.
Then the will read, "To my nephew Irving,
who always wanted to be mentioned in my will,
'Hello, Irving!'"

A woman called her doctor and said,
"Doctor, my dog just swallowed 50 Bufferins,
what shall I do?"
The doctor said, "What else?
Give him a headache!"

☆ ☆ ☆

There is a guy having trouble with his rear end.
He can't get a doctor to help him.
He can't find a drug store open or a doctor.
A friend of his says, "Look,
my grandmother used to have a cure for this."
He says, "Get a bunch of tea leaves,
boil them, stick them around your rear end
till you get to a doctor.
"The guy goes to see his proctologist
Monday morning.
He forgot to take away the tea leaves.
The doctor examines his rear end.
He says,
"I see that you're going to make
a long ocean voyage!"

Personally, I'm against political jokes.
Too often they get elected to office!

Three men were finalists in a spelling bee.
On the final day they were told
they would have to supply the right word
in a phrase and spell it correctly.
The phrase was,
"Old MacDonald had a. ..."
The Israeli guy said,
"Old MacDonald had a kibbutz."
He was told that he spelled the word correctly,
but it was not the correct one.
The Russian guy said,
"Old MacDonald had a commune."
He was also told
that he spelled the word correctly,
but that it was not the correct one.
The Polish guy said,
"Old MacDonald had a
E-I-E-I-O."

★ ★ ★

Do you know what mixed emotions are?
It's when you see your mother-in-law
drive over a cliff in your new Cadillac!

He thinks High Cholesterol is a Jewish Holiday.

‡‡‡

Guy goes to a doctor for a physical.
When said physical is concluded
the doctor says, "You're in terrific shape,
especially for a 58-year-old man."
The guy counters with,
"Who told you I'm 58?
I'm 75, and I feel great!"
The doctor then says, "That's wonderful.
I must ask you,
how old was your father when he died?"
"Who told you my father died?
He's 99-years-old
and in better shape than I am."
"Marvelous! Could you tell me
how old your grandfather was when he died?"
"Who told you my grandfather died?
He's 123-years-old, in great shape,
and last week he got married."
"That's amazing – 123-years-old
and he still wanted to get married?"
"Who told you he wanted to get married?"

††††

As a comedian
he has a repertoire of six jokes
all told – and told – and told!

‡‡‡

Three women at a Hadassah dinner....
One says, "My husband bought me an estate
in Mt. Kisco, New York."
The other woman says,
"I have a beautiful home up in Rye."
The third woman, who lives in the Bronx, says,
"I live three stations from Scarsdale!"

A woman called the Police Department
and said,
"I have a sex maniac in my apartment.
Pick him up in the morning."

†††

A guy says to another guy,
"How many times have you been married?"
He answers, "Twice."
"What happened to your first wife?"
"She fell in a wishing well."
"I didn't know they worked!"

☆ ☆ ☆

As a conductor,
he doesn't know his brass from his oboe.

A dentist who was having a romance
with one of his married women patients
said to her,
"Darling, we've got to stop seeing each other;
you're down to your last tooth!"

☎

A middle-aged lady goes to a doctor.
After she's undressed he says,
"Lady, that's the ugliest body I've ever seen."
She sighs and says,
"That's what *my* doctor told me."
"What did you come to me for?"
She says, "I wanted to get another opinion."

▷◁

There was a mix-up
at the swank Fifth Avenue florist shop.
Wrong cards were attached
to two imposing floral wreaths.
The one that went to a druggist
moving to a new building read,
"Deepest sympathy."
The one intended for the funeral
of a leading banker read,
"Good luck in your new location."

↓🔨

This guy tells his psychiatrist that he's gay.
The doctor asks if anyone else
in the family is gay.
The guy says, "Yes, my three brothers."
The doc says, "Who else?"
The guy says, "My father."
The doc says, "Who else?"
The guy says, "Some of my cousins."
The doc asks,
"Doesn't anyone in your family like girls?"
The guy says, "Sure, my sister."

Two guys in a gym —
one guy is putting a girdle on.
His friend says,
"Since when are you wearing a girdle?"
He says, "Since my wife found it
in the glove compartment of my car!"

♦♦♦

A man goes to a psychiatrist —
the psychiatrist says to the man,
"What do you do for a living?"
He says, "I'm an auto mechanic."
The psychiatrist says, "Get under the couch."

☆ ☆ ☆

A fellow had won a million dollars
in the sweepstakes.
The only one who knew that he had won
was the agent who had sold him the ticket.
Knowing that the winner had a heart condition,
the agent was afraid to inform him
of his good luck.
So he went to the man's doctor and said,
"Your patient just won a million dollars
in the sweepstakes.
I know he is a cardiac case,
and I am afraid to tell him.
Something could happen to him.
Tomorrow, while you are examining him,
inadvertently tell him that he won
a million dollars in the sweepstakes
and if anything happens to him,
you are right there."
Next day, while examining the patient,
the doctor said to him,
"Oh, by the way,
you won a million dollars in the sweepstakes."
"I did?
Doctor, I'm gonna give you half."
And with that the doctor dropped dead.

☆ ☆ ☆

A man met the ex-president, Nixon.
He says, "Mr. President,
with all these problems you had
how do you sleep at night?"
Mr. Nixon says,
"I sleep like a baby.
I cry a little,
I wet the bed a little!"

Betcha you can't tell me why
they call language "the mother tongue?".....
It's because
father never gets a chance to use it.

☆ ⭐ ☆

A man walked into an insurance office
and said "I'd like to get my life insured."
The agent said, "Do you drive a car?"
The man said, "No, I don't."
Then he asked,
"Do you fly a plane?"
and again the answer was no.
The insurance agent said,
"I'm sorry, Sir,
but we no longer insure pedestrians!"

A fellow tries to cross the Mexican border
on his bicycle.
He's got two big bags on his shoulder.
The guard says,
"What's in the bags?"
He says, "Sand."
The guard says,
"Get them off – we'll examine them."
The fellow takes the two bags off,
they empty them out,
they look through them,
and find nothing but sand.
The guy puts the sand back in the bags,
puts the bags back on his shoulders,
and the little fellow crosses the border
on his bicycle.
Every two weeks for six months this goes on.
Finally one week the fellow didn't show up,
and the guard meets him downtown.
He says, "Buddy, you had us crazy.
We knew you were smuggling something.
I won't say anything....
what were you smuggling?"
The guy says, "Bicycles."

A couple checked into a hotel
in Pittsburgh next to the railroad station.
They got the only room left in town.
The man goes out to visit some friends.
His wife lays down to take a rest.
A train goes by so fast that the vibration
knocks her out of bed and onto the floor.
Ten minutes later another train goes by
and knocks her to the floor.
Ten minutes later another train goes by
and knocks her to the floor.
She calls the manager.
She explains and says
"what kind of place is this?
The vibrations of the train
knocked me out of bed and on to the floor."
He said, "I don't believe you."
He does.
She says, "lay down on the bed for a minute."
He does.
Just then the husband comes in and says,
"what s going on here?"
Manager says,
"believe it or not, I'm waiting for a train."

★ ★ ★

Two drunks walking along Broadway
in New York.
One goes down into the subway by mistake.
He comes up the other entrance,
and his friend is waiting for him.
The waiting drunk says,
"Where were you?"
The other one says,
"I was in some guy's basement.
Has he got a set of trains!"

☎

O'Malley went to confession one day
and told the priest that he had made love
ten times the night before.
The priest said,
"O'Malley, I'm surprised at you.
Tell me now, was it a married woman?"
And O'Malley said,
"Oh sure, Father, it was my wife."
"But, O'Malley, you don't have to confess
making love to your wife."
"I know, Father,
but I just had to tell *somebody.*

A jury was out for seventy-two hours.
When they came back into the courtroom,
the judge said,
"Have you come to a decision?"
"Yes, your honor,"
replied the foreman.
"We decided not to become involved."

▷◁